BEFORE RECOLLECTION

PRINCETON SERIES OF CONTEMPORARY POETS
FOR OTHER BOOKS IN THE SERIES, SEE PAGE 74

Before Recollection

ANN LAUTERBACH

PRINCETON UNIVERSITY PRESS

Copyright © 1987 by Princeton University Press
Published by Princeton University Press, 41 William Street,
Princeton, New Jersey 08540
In the United Kingdom: Princeton University Press,
Guildford, Surrey

All Rights Reserved
Library of Congress Cataloging in Publication Data will be
found on the last printed page of this book

ISBN 0-691-06698-1
    0-691-01437-X (pbk.)

Publication of this book has been aided by a grant from
the Paul Mellon Fund of Princeton University Press

This book has been composed in Linotron Bembo

Clothbound editions of Princeton University Press books are
printed on acid-free paper, and binding materials are chosen
for strength and durability. Paperbacks, although
satisfactory for personal collections, are not usually
suitable for library rebinding

Printed in the United States of America by
Princeton University Press
Princeton, New Jersey

ACKNOWLEDGMENTS

Acknowledgment is made to the following publications, in which the poems in this book originally appeared:

Paris Review: "Still," "Betty Observed," "Naming the House," "Graffiti"

Forum: "Bridgehampton 1950, 1980"

Niagara Magazine: "The Walled Palace"

Conjunctions: "Holding Air," "Away, with Jane Bowles," "As Far as the Eye Can See," "Café Acute," "Like Attracts," "Still Life with Apricots," "Closing Hours," "Monody," "Path," "Subject to Change," "Aperture," "Coastal," "October Lake," "Moonrise, Rain," "Sacred Weather"

Seneca Review: "Narrow Margins," "In the Garden"

Pequod: "Saint Lucia"

Mothers of Mud: "Mimetic"

New York Arts Journal: "Landscape with Vase," "Before Recollection"

Brooklyn Review: "Where I Am," "Approaching the Panorama," "Maple, Moon, Jay," "The Meadow," "The Chamber"

American Poetry Review: "Here and There"

SoHo Arts Weekly: "Like Moths to Flame"

Partisan Review: "Second Descent, Again"

Appearances: "Poem for Margrit, for Frida"

Mudfish: "Day Dreams of Night," "Medieval Evening," "Inner Life"

Poetry in Motion: "Almost"

Poetry New York: "Vernal Elegy"

Artforum: "The Vanquished"

"Transcendental Postcard," "Moonlight in Calais," "Portrait," "Later That Evening," "Some Other Time," "Topaz," and "A Simple Service" appeared in *Later That Evening*, published by Jordan Davies. "Carousel" was published in *Aerial*, an anthology conceived by Yvonne Jacquette and edited by Edwin Denby. "Psyche's Dream" appeared first in *Epoch* and again in *Ecstatic Occasions, Expedient Forms*, an anthology on form edited by David Lehman. *Sacred Weather* was first published as a sequence by the Grenfell Press. "An Aura of Abstraction Gives Way," "Platonic Subject," and "Lake of Isles" here appear for the first time in print.

For BC
and for Peter Straub

CONTENTS

I. NAMING THE HOUSE

II. AS FAR AS THE EYE CAN SEE

III. PSYCHE'S DREAM

IV. A SIMPLE SERVICE

I. NAMING THE HOUSE

Still

The sleeping urgencies are perhaps ruined now
In the soul's haphazard sanctuary,
Ignored like a household
Dormant in the landscape, a backwoods dump
Where the last care has worn through its last
Memory. We might think of this as a blessing
As we thrash in the nocturnal waste:
Rubble of doors, fat layers of fiber
Drooping under eaves, weeds
Leaning in lassitude after heavy rain
Has surged from a whitened sky.
Thunder blooms unevenly in unknowable places
Breaking distance into startling new chambers
We cannot enter; potentially, a revelation.

Deep Midnight, a song on the Chinese zither.
This must be long after the storm, long
After the revolution. It seems some things
Were kept in storage after all: cool air
Quietly throbbing, a few candles, chance songs
"Soul to soul" on the radio. Chance is a variant
Of change, the weather changing, chancy
But destined. Our trust is that we, too, are
Forms attached to content, content to meanings
Aroused. It is our custom to bring things about.

Bridgehampton 1950, 1980

Garden, hedge, pool,
Planned to guard the old line, define
And compose the imagination's brown capacity.
Our extent is more than memory
Or the text of a poem willed to the wall
Although our tenacious forebears whisper
Collections, passed from father to son to son
While mother prunes.
                        The earth, mulched,
Gives back a frenzied design
And fish hatch at the feet of toads.
I know these roads, this cascade of vine
Heavy with wine never to be drunk
Unless a parade of girls in white socks
Tramples, and the sheets are stained
With rituals only girls observe:
Ophelia once again prepared with tansy's
Bitterness. An endowment of Queen Anne's lace,
Paths around the butternut; tarragon, basil, mint.
A rare magnolia blooms before an early autumn death.
The pond was splattered with lilies like wet paint.

Transcendental Postcard

The outlook such that time is told on waking,
Without aid of cock or clock's crow.
In fact all the birds are elsewhere,
Poised on glossy page or in some fall
Migration. Sun up over mountain is precision,
Then mist travels, exhaling day.
All else, all change, is air,
Dew relenting on the blades
And mirror rhymes
Where water bears resemblance:
A strut of hues to pale even Revlon's alchemy and,
In the center of its glaze, a cauldron of sky-cast blue.

Moonlight in Calais

This is the first scene.
A recondite setting but plentiful, autumnal.
There is a sense of circularity, many forms of rind,
And tiny pink peculiarities which you name.
I arrive on time, expected but strange.
We have never discussed omens
But there are flames to induce imaginings.
Evening. Each in his or her own
Elegy gown, we curl by the fire
With antique dice and board, turn gossip
To fate. Later, we check for birds
But the blue heron does not visit this time.

Then the slow day makes clear there is a circle;
Distance is obtained. The pond
Alleviates our need for limits
And is man-made. Elsewhere,
Beyond the ridge, there are stores, farmlands.
I know I am under your roof, see
Stripes of mundane pink in the evening sky
Just before you allow a thin moon to shine.
At the end of the play there is a murder or a marriage.

Betty Observed

A tinted, unnecessary warmth coils
Loosely around us, adding to the noiseless shambles
We had no time to predict, so that recovery
As in "speedy," as in autumn's cool sweep,
Appears at its most fictive, the way
Our heroine is, spending most of her day
In front of the mirror. Please identify with her.
She is lovely, Victorian, her auburn hair, upswept,
Held by tortoise-shell pins and silver combs;
Moonstones hang, drop by drop, from her ears
And throat. The rest of her has the voluptuous
Lacy pale look of dried hydrangea. Her hands
Innocent, but craving; clearly, she is skilled,
At needlepoint, or paint. By now we should be
Spellbound and impatient, wishing she would do
Or say something. When I was young, I used to
Check pages for talk; dialogue was the key
To readability. That was before I had a taste
For abstraction. "I love you Betty" was a good sign,
And big words pointing wildly at no time or place
Like toy compasses agitating with uncertainties
Were few, and far between. "I love you too, Edward."

The Walled Palace

In the hierarchy of the day we are made agile,
Persuade ourselves to play-down generation,
Pause in mapping out. They met
Under a table in Mexico. The drums beat wildly
As long-legged birds—those ashtray birds—
Strutted, raved. The flea market
Has these things for sale, so next day
Only fragments are reclaimed.
"My husband is my drummer *and* my band leader."

Sometimes to say is to have
So we can pass from the room empty-handed.
Concurrently, there are things to see:
A band of windows and, beyond,
Tall conical trees that winter green.
At best things are untidy, latent, fugitive.
Words fail where no present is
And we age in our own narration.
We are, Pascal said, so unwise
As to wander in times to which we don't belong,
Choose *seraglio* over other possibilities, other homes.

Holding Air

The day's accuracies, however feeble, are not
Domestic although the line they draw
Is encumbered, possibly even daunted
By that smudge I know is a river.
And now you know it as it slides
Onto the sky, an unguent soothing the horizon.
You care also to know who you are.
Nothing so much as view but more than noise,
For the hum pertains to you, fanning the interior
And entering here through the window's screen.
I had forgotten this attenuated lapse
Between us, a sort of moat spun around us
As we collapse from day to day,
Each of us ammunition for the other and
For the night. The rope on the low roof
Is strung like a hammock holding air,
Doubling back on itself, limp,
Catching a glimpse of sun better than the water.
Here it comes again, the light
Reined in, riding that rope from wall to wall.

9

An Aura of Abstraction Gives Way

Good rentals. Market for ice skates, skull caps,
Lake view flurries where dark
Takes up slack in winter, hit-or-miss splendor,
Flash lit. You could say "christened rain,"
Pelt-on-roof absorbing touch, more-or-less skin deep
Snow down from the north to the mouth of a river.

Money problems. The title of one of his songs,
Revival of urban scores: I forget how it feels
To be rich, create an impression
By hurling chocolate cake across a crowded room.
Love-sick Californian, or just a vendetta?
Fat cat curls on a heap of sunlight.
Did you say *personal* space? Not much.

Ice froze amuck, hacked-off limbs, cloven weight.
Imagine an arm ripped out bloodless.
Oracular doom gives way to real life,
Art fills the artifice: crimson limb
Paints out the horizon, no place takes place,
Limbo star, moon. Good night for truck rentals,
Highways rutted and aflame: antlers ride heads
Ride racks; decor sales at pit stops, diamond decals,
Knick-knack guns. Good days for bad deals
As candor steps out to let things pass,
Traffic tied up for scene: some woman escaping success
Hit by a cab midtown. Record year for settings,

Lamé threads pilfered from Egypt's tombs,
Atavistic carriages emerge from scrim: dragon lady,
Princeling, a quartet of undercover cops at barnyard door
Waiting to hatch perfect cruelties, stamp on all eggs
Golden or just plain white until paramedics arrive
To sweep up shells, snow, the great limb blooming across.

Away, with Jane Bowles

Going away is often a formal statement of intent.
There she was in Paris in 1950 in love
With the river and theatre and shoes, but dreaming
Of Tangiers and the dunes. She loved the mirage.
I do too, although I dream of you, in color,
And of furnished curves like cakes layered with decor,
Rooms cut from the landscape, a relocated interior.
Is a dream a mirage and therefore literature
And does it have intent? I am in Minneapolis
Where there are lakes and a river, but the river
Is somehow absent: a thin slice, a narrow cut.
We are waiting for winter, the main character
In this place, big and crazed as the bus driver who,
Hurtling across the bridge, called, "We are going to do
The same to Bob and to Fuller!" The moon was full,
A harvest of light falling on the fallen leaves,
The only excess. Who is Bob and who is Fuller
And what is to be done by winter? There she was
In Paris in 1950 hoping to untie habits, visiting Alice,
Unable to write, eating Alice's cakes. Here I am
In Minneapolis where everything is pitched
At vernacular sight: a stray cat, a kid on a bike,
An old woman talks about milk as autumn
Rides away like a car, a departing place.
This is where intention finds us and breaks, as water
Breaks over the edge to be absorbed into the earth's
Deep syntax: Jane's mirage, my dream, winter's coming acts.

Naming the House

The ample, plain snow inhibits detail
But frees splendor briefly, completely,
Like a dream ornamented with a consoling retrieval:
Balsam gathered at the top of the stairs
At the Chappaqua house. And I think
Of how we might walk out onto the pond
Unknowingly, cross the slight curb
Onto ice, trusting similitude's throw of white.
And I think also of how women, toward evening,
Watch as the buoyant dim slowly depletes
Terrain, and frees the illuminated house
So we begin to move about, reaching for potholders
And lids, while all the while noting
That the metaphor of the house is ours to keep
And the dark exterior only another room
Waiting for its literature.
She dallies now in plots
But feels a longing for dispersal,
For things all to succumb to the night's snow
Omitting and omitting. She has this attention:
To the reticent world enforced by the sensual
And her curiosity, a form of anticipation,
Knowing the failure of things to null and knowing, too,
The joy of naming it this, and this is mine.

Narrow Margins

We have leafed through these margins enough to know
They are not vacations, but absence readied
Not unlike a young girl on her way to bed
In a strange place, a narrow sky
Hung with cares and lies on unseen ropes
And held by a system of passions.
Here all is renovated, enclosed.
What once passed as dream
(Those candid dragons, fed on Ajax,
Who flew nightly beyond the curve of fate)
Turns one day into a wrought-iron gate
strapped with fat red bouquets and unsigned notes.

Death is not simple; it starts a process.
Later, she moves to L.A. He flies south.
She phones for zip codes and news.
Just before dinner he excused himself, went
Somewhat unwell to bed where he grew cold
And awkward, too awkward to be asleep.
The morgue is closed for the holidays.
There are cards, four deep, across the mantlepiece.
The poet gives a performance in which he is an owl.
The photographer gives a talk on how long color lasts.
The year ends. We are forced to the place of amazement.

II. AS FAR AS THE EYE CAN SEE

Saint Lucia

1.

Suppose it is enough: rock, tree, sky,
These uncounted, unaccountable surfaces.
And suppose this is the entrance
Among these hills
That sound high, far-off, look old,
Hooded, sloped, ending with an owl, a cup.
Through lime slit leaves
Light travels, a rag.
There are tangles everywhere, and salt.
Under the leg of a chair, its rim half-shining.
The sea in the distance, its rim half-shining.

2.

Not quite fledged the surfaces change
More-or-less dangerous, as if
Partly digested or not yet evolved.
Tuesday; o'clock.
Direction is peripheral,
A shapeless vicinity cast by net.
Light is a rag. Leaf, bird, that.
Silence, rescinded as wings,
Marries air to yellowness.
There are dictions here
That adhere to necessity, to speech not said.

3.

Between the ominous and transcendent sea,
Each present as light determines,
Are insignias: triangles at large, passings.

Everything is wordless but palpable.
The harbor with its vessels.
The sky with its slow baggage.
The mind with its vessels, its baggage.
Clouds come from the same direction
Slowly over the hills, encumbered passengers.
There is nothing between us
But the play of these various casual leaves.

4.

The sea, solitary or not,
Implies the confines of a dream.
I'm between Beckett and Bishop,
The one entirely in, the other there
Civilizing Brazil, clarity to clarity.
I'd rather be a fishwife or a frog,
A secretary taking dictation.
Do this. Do that.
Respite from the brave and intent.
The mango I ate under that flat-leafed tree
Tastes better than any imagined thing,
Salt erased by sweet
Intoxicating, solitary, a tongue within.

5.

Dipping back to gather some quality,
Not the stone but the color of the stone
As it travels, light's motif,
To land on the rim of a cup.

The words might be seen
Lying here on the beach
Complete and distinct in sameness.
And I have kept you with me
As a version of nearness
To say what I am kept from saying
Here, on the beach, with stones piled up.

    6.
The drone flies up to take a queen.
He dies ecstatic, founding an empire.
Such aspiration! Such requital!
When things get crowded she leaves,
Takes up home in a cave
With a swarm of workers and eunuch drones.
The hummingbird has been each day
To stick its long thing into the blooms.
Conrad says, "the mere incidents of the surface,
The reality, the reality I tell you fades."
Light is delayed on the opaque leaves.

    7.
Or suppose not.
A cup is not an inlet.
The hours climb up the hunch-backed hills.
Thursday; o'clock.
The owl has its habits.
Everything seems random, diffuse,
As images collect
Into some quality, as of surfaces intact.

The lizard visits twilight
Down one leg of a chair, across the porch.
The hills end with passage, a cup, a call.

8.
They clamor to get out; rat, rag, owl,
The hummingbird, its radiant stick,
And the three-note call.
The hens are parading and dull.
Leaves keep moving; they want to be winged.
The syntax of solitude is
To witness versions that clock and petal,
Enfolding instances. Among these hills
That are high, far-off, hooded, old,
Sloped, ending with a cup.
The thing is handed to us. We hand it back.
In the diction of surfaces, a distinguished absence.

In the Garden

The view is partial and has always been
In deference to what lies ahead:
Some version of next, a shelf
Packed with trophies from a minor war,
Winter's end. On the flight back the sky
Was visually unconscious,
A vast impairment as when recollection
Blinds the whole with a single storm;
Hours formed into days, weeks and years
Lost to this impasto mask we travel through.
The view is partial. Today, slow and bright
In spots, it crests and falls apart, melting.
I have in my mind's eye an ancestral place
Thick with iris, lily, tulip,
Whose high grass, parted by a path, I
Never saw but which she painted, sitting out
On the lawn, in late spring, everything seen.

As Far as the Eye Can See

Perhaps the weather has nothing to say
Other than the simple duress of cause and effect
We muster into forbearance,
So little of which is left it takes on desire
As when reticence reaches its limit,
Signals an embrace. The wind is favorable
Even as it thrashes the stipulating tree
Into panic, an urgency beyond its means,
Reminding us of how much better it would be
To know less and therefore not impart meaning
To things left well enough alone.
This the weather never does
And is why all the turbulent paintings
Only suggest the carriage of light
Mattering everywhere, or the rain, stricken,
Conversing with familiar distances of earth.
And now I wonder if intimacy is tonal,
Some agreement of parts along the surface
Weather, refusing to rest, narrates
With all the clarity words might articulate to us.

Café Acute

Having found your method, you scrape
For a softer alarm, dilute clarion orange
To peach and the possible calm that fruit is.
But the season, without leverage,
Spoils to a residue of images
Parched, grounded, so you paint hands
Clasped to hands of those you never will meet
Even at the new café which smells of disinfectant.

My method is to scan for something to announce.
With the river as guide
I wait while the excursion crosses
To the brick interior, angled for blindness.
The harbor, in another neighborhood patch, is
More storied and gently inclined for arrival.
I see now fragmentary reds of sleeve
Or scarf, some glad foreboding, and,
Before it crashes,
A huge white wave coiled in the inward sea.

Mimetic

Recumbent against any mirror, any stardom,
Dazed to be included, at last, in the night,
You imitate day stretched across a beach
Noted by those of us for whom the sea is reflective
But is the sea a film of the sea, ageless?

Seventeen, a mime. This is one way to hide
Lack of authenticity, although style
Carries clout in crowd scenes.
You have painted your toenails Car Hop Pink,
A clear choice against the sky's transience.

The sea mimes the sea. It seems ageless,
Whichever hues the waves hit.
Her face, projected on a screen,
Records the gaze of our capitulation.
Gene Tierney walks along the cliffs, reflective.

Pavese said sentiment, in art, is accuracy,
But the poem would not stretch
To phrase the red cliffs, the seizure of place.
You see the world as self. For us, she
Is world, enduring, veracity of was
Being what is. We cannot look
At what we love without failure,
The failure of the world to reflect itself.

Like Attracts

A rag, I thought, and then, revived,
Settled for fire
Less than what matters but enough
To entail metaphor and therefore what I think
I am. For a while choice seems infinite
Until I pass under the boughs
Where the cardinal, a flame in flight,
Has alighted. A brief alliance takes place
Against what we know to be the case:
Your instinct for gambling; my threshold.

If the mood were to settle
And we were to live in this place,
This huge room where walls are pines
And the pool, also receptive, allows glimpses,
However brief, of endurance
(No more than a creature that swims
Out of its depth) then these visitors
Who tour their own sex would be less shrill
And the crimson flight of evening ours, and still.

Landscape with Vase

Predatory, then, or rushed,
Self breaks into categories of self:
Here flies away, here waits, here resembles
Ancient tenacities of fruit
And of the sorrow of petals:

Collapsed, partial, redolent, wet.
And I could say such moments contract
When it enters another phase
And is consumed, as the bloom
Opens to full stature and brands emptiness

Crowding it out.
Now it diminishes like a remote era
Seemingly irrelevant, not knowing
The faith of disciples,
How they wept when it faltered

And went about barefoot, unseemly, detached.
Definition pares down. A slow cloud
Lifts light off the grass and slides it
Downhill to where the roses are.
Things take on the look of potential:

A mild shadow is sometimes consoling
And might lead to stillness, simple containment.

Portrait

Let's say it is fundamental, not derived
From approach, alchemy, or lust:
A design, instinctive as an oval.
And let's say we are in the process
Of finding out what's left
When brilliance is torn from the day,
The masterpiece replaced
On the wall of its origin
And all these vases emptied into gardens.

To the left, trapped,
A wavering stretch of leaves and, right,
A chord of recessions far from arm's reach:
Bar, ledge, roof, sill, bridge,
Beyond which the river
Upholds the course of events. Enthralled,
Time gangs up, as in "whereabouts unknown"
And the forsaken steps through, a matador
Limping after the kill, drunk,
The entire retrospective unfurled in his cape.

Among insects there must be portraits too,
Even those that do not flinch or spill.
A page of musical notes
Flares while the head turns, lips brushed wet.

Platonic Subject

Momentum and wash of the undefined,
as if clarity fell through the sieve of perception,
announced as absence of image.
But here is a twig in the form of a wishbone.
Aroused, I take it, and leave its outline
scarred in snow which the sun will later heal:
form of the real melts back into the ideal
and I have a twig.

Where I Am

No longer enchantment but slowed or slowly held
Nocturnes hummed through the arch of ceremony.
There are lunar variations and lovers,
Now and then, limber enough.
They do not talk in night air. For days
I am elevated among them, suffering variation:

Honeymooning, enraged.
The ballroom where I am harms.
Ellipses lap, giving the floor this scope.
Someone drapes the sleeve of an imperishable gown:
Layers of white, layers of deceit.
Gestures of a mime are held in check.

If only, lyrical, overtakes the dawn.
Voluptuous shades fall into a hunched-up song.
A piano sits behind the curtains:
Miniature keys, miniature recluse.
Enchanted, I come to listen, eager to hear,
But on the wedding lawn a huge man

Admires my wide, brimmed hat.
Passive as silk, he takes me to the garden,
Not the apse. He is scared and knows it,
Spits into the rose. I have seen him drum his legs.
I have heard him talk about his toys.
I have seen him pull the cat up by the tail.

What persists? Today, balanced by habit,
Is exactly in place, and the grays, always musical,

Mutate choice ordained by cloud.
Words might recover their sway, shored up
Against perpendiculars, but
Light's grip is accidental, wherever it rests.

I wear a wardrobe of birds, heirloom wings, talons.
Now the heron tempts me to believe
All things named are immanent. These leaves
Swirl upward from the simple task of water;
The river is fastened by the radiance of a shield.
A margin of dread meets a margin of wonder,

A scaffold of terror and allure.
Layers of rain will age the view.
Some days there are no sails and some sail by
Inhabited, but the column of sky is
Architectural, burdened with its air.
Later, encrusted on either side, towering stars.

Approaching the Panorama

Maples, reticent, in a hush of russet and rose
Attracting their opposites, and the ice coast
Recedes along a curve coded below the surface
And robins are back working the pervious
And the wild cherry grapples:
A blind drawing, animated, nervous.
                                        A thaw,
And the temptation to fib, to say
The bouillabaisse is perfect,
To say all the legendary teachers were women,
To say it doesn't matter, really.
Pale blades appear under snow.
For some, country life is disastrous,
A false provision inspiring truths
Lyrically applied: O bold storm! O myriad sky!
While those of use who abide the city
Scatter, learning unnatural efficiencies
And fearing we are on the brink of maturity.
We give flowers for diligence.
Our pace is traffic: heads bowed, shoulders
Ever guarded against chemistry.
Here, the spillway is unabated only in dream.
O flock of wild blue birds descending!

Graffiti

Callow and *amorphous*, not gods
But adjectives flung at the sun
Whose hot fibers protest their distance
Lovingly, touching our skulls lovingly.
This is not a desert.
This is a place where a pedestrian stops,
Thinking the face in the window is an owl's.
The face in the window is a Renaissance Youth
Eternally snivelling under a green umbrella.
Across the street, it is written DRUNK DOOM
In large bold, short-circuiting the STIFLED,
DROWSY, UNIMPASSIONED GRIEF I remember in London.
Much of London I don't recall, although names
Sail back to me on small craft, like plunder.
Loss of names is one kind of leakage
But there is another: the actual scale
Breezing along in daring episodes,
Most of it escaping utterance, falling
Back into the temple housing *callow* and *amorphous*
as well as *enchanted*, and there waits
To be spirited toward us, away from the unrecovered.

Still Life with Apricots

Tones implausibly migrate. This is no phantom slide
Into proximity, but a shadow whose brevity
Is deployed as the capacity to linger.
There is a mute obligation for implements
To recall gesture, although those which hold
Hold only the lipped curvature of shelter,
Its brevity waylaid, luminous.
Bulbs, tips of prongs, ripeness;
Heavily humped spheres perpetually darken.
Surprised from oblivion, a stem
Rests indelibly. Each topic is a surface
Ingrained and potential, a reverie emptied,
A breach drawn easily, singularly. Tones
Shift across a slab like the boundaries of grief.

A field abounding in new orders of discrepancy,
Casually alert, filtered, departing
From the communal nave.
Beauty is a way of meriting surprise,
A renewal while remembering how the table is set,
The formal feeling engaged by stasis, recognition.
It occurs to us to do something else
While small births continue, followed by
Celebratory dreams. Looking around, we feel
A sleepy desire to arrange things differently
Since what is reflected is never the same anyway.
Freesia, gin, apricots are passed across
The mutant glare into edges and shapes. Edges,
Shapes remind us of solitary inclusion: how each must wait.

III. PSYCHE'S DREAM

Here and There

Today I wake having swung, naked, in London,
At the ambassador's house. What happened?
Baseball fever, Fassbinder, the need to undress
After something French.
Tonight, also, will have a remittance.
Here is a crowd of angels from Padua,
One gold, one red, the others obscured
Apart from their heads which, profiled, stare forward.
Mary is returning from her nuptial rite.
She is kept from the rest
By blue, and her hand grips her robe
So that a dark arch forms just below the waist.
I'll dream white, pull curtains apart, see a kid's face.

We almost escape narration and, after the war,
The noise our brothers made we did not hear.
There were remnants of a garden
Where the landscape dipped
And old flowers grew wild
Around stone relics of a birdbath.
Those were the days: stones, relics, fates,
Slow passage of color through leaf
And fear incited by fluorescent clocks at night.
We used to have a reputation for reality,
And now these. What happened? Mist
Is rising off the river; a low boat slides by.
Up ahead: the androgyny of winter
When all things seek gray, and the great star
Chills us back into dreams under late and later dawns.

Later That Evening

Wood laid in for the winter; the rest of the century.
"I used to know everything about fish,"
He claimed, staring at the flame
On the mast of the gondola,
Its miniature gold hull afloat on the table.
"Skate fish, blows, sea thrush
And rare heart of bass
We used to fish at the Vineyard, summers."
A silent film called *Snow* is shown at the window.
"This is bliss for me," she offered,
"This absence." Outside, something exhaled
And the surprised birds sang to it.
Midnight dawn; eternal preamble.
And the real world? There, where the ʹestate
Of the imagined ends: trees cut up, fishbones left.

Carousel

To embark it lifts, flies up, scans the view:
The river, slit between highway and sky;
The sky, a distant plinth
Set between deckle-edged bricks.
She likes the way it comes out of the blue.
Inside, petals are temporarily blazed,
Light as Japanese sleeves in the wind.
Those were purple, dye of purple herbs
Brushed on silk, unpluckable, walking across.
"Won't the guards see you wave your sleeves to me?"

Nevertheless she is afraid.
She does not know how to cross paths and stop.
Images keep her awake, waiting.
What comes out of the blue? Why smile?
There it flies low over inclined fields,
A dossier of wings. Elsewhere,
An outline on a box indicating prowess.
She gets the binoculars out to see up close.
Copper pans are dusty on the wall
And she is full of tears, the dread of tears.

Above the river: an outline of smokestacks.
They could be set to music or dance,
But she is waiting for the mist to rise.
Her wish? Carnal, flamboyant. A landscape
Charged, noisy, dangerous,
Faintly dangerous as she crosses the street.
She knows things spread, shadow enlarging image,

Illicit perceptions of blue mornings, gentian evenings.
Altering goes on, even on days that are mostly night,
And she is rapt, watching, almost heraldic.

All across the country the hero peers
Uneasily over the shoulder of a girl.
She has never been away, is full of tears,
Dread of tears. She mentions her father.
Tennis whites, weekend admirers,
Trips back from Japan with silk kimonos.
"Once, I picked a lily from the pond
And was stung by bees." The horses
Are all in a circle. Music begins.
She sits on the red smiling horse and waits to ascend.

This spell is too real to be broken.
Have some nuts. Have some chedder cheese.
The caprice is his, his sudden entrances
And willowy lies strapped into rhymes, bouquets.
He comes down the aisle wearing vestments.
She receives his blessing, is given
Dominion over events, the right to tell stories.
"I ride through the sky to the place
That houses beginnings. I fly
As the crow, as the snow, as smoke, as wind."

Another pal from college dies
Leaving us unchanged, but fewer.
Her secret is the only one left, and so wanted.
Early that morning the wind absorbed him.
His will rose and departed, taking her with it.
And certainly she saw it rise from the pond

While the woman stood aside, modest as death.
To recollect is to choose. The event
Sets music in motion; the horse
Rises and falls in its circular path.

I like masks, deeper shades of blue,
How it concludes black.
A swimmer is adorned with one arm
Rising out of the blue.
A man in the sea.
A painting of a man in the sea.
I like the way it comes out of the blue.
The horse rises and falls; my sleeves are waving.
It is not dark that scares me, but the limit
Which places the house in the field, the horse in its stall.

A bald supple surface falls between cracks
As the door slowly opens.
Light is one way to wake up, image another,
But she must tiptoe across the floor
To tell her secret. The floor is cold.
She does not know how to say it.
We must invent a new mood,
Gargoyles, scents, purple-robed figures
Walking the courtyard.
The horse did not fly up. The horse is wingless.

Those who never loved him say
He was witness to dust, shelter of his hours,
Among the faithless, faithless.
They cannot see in the dark.
We are gregarious, blind dolls.

41

Over her shoulder, the painting depicts will.
Staring at the view, she has a sense of place
And of omission. The ways in which we live
Are earmarked for letting go, and so
She makes her descent, plucks it, rises into the blue.

Psyche's Dream

If dreams could dream, beyond the canon of landscapes
Already saved from decorum, including mute
Illicit girls cowering under eaves
Where the books are stacked and which they
Pillage, hoping to find not events but response

If dreams could dream, free from the damp crypt
And from the bridge where she went
To watch the spill and the tree
Standing on its head, huge and rootless
(Of which the wasp is a cruel illustration

Although its sting is not), the decay
Now spread into the gardens, their beds
Tethered to weeds and to all other intrusions;
Then the perishing house, lost from view
So she must, and you, look out to see
Not it but an image of it, would be

Nowhere and would not resemble, but would languish
On the other side of place where the winged boy
Touches her ear far from anywhere
But gathered like evening around her waist
So that within each dream is another, remote
And mocking and a version of his mouth on her mouth.

Some Other Time

Where was I? Sailing through yesterday's argument
For the uncluttered look, or beseeching my master
To untie my left wrist? This time of year
Is humbling: after the explosion and fame of leaves
Comes this tawdry mess that augurs a month of tasks.
We are also here in some accumulation,
As of leaves, or distance,
But your reference is to things near:
A small wind disturbs a bonfire.
Perhaps nuance is unnecessary
But this small wind
Varies the yield: not a full dissolution
Although the flames sting and batter a tepid sky.
But where was I? In California
Among dry bright things that decorate the desert
And stub out billowing contours of dream.
Even the squirrels are unfamiliar.
The highest part is light, access
Made by footholds in aquamarine, hard-edge pools
That jilt the sun's façade. There are legends here
And speed, as if speed could get you somewhere else.

Do all cowboys slang their way to heaven in fecund jeans?
This blond phenomenon, this trap in the wings,
The way the straight man is now
Afraid of his shadow, much less his girl.
Is it for lack of seashells that panic pervades?
Or is it those skinny dogs up there in the hills
Mocking their prey's alarm? It is, as they say,

A fool's paradise where even desire is on call or purpose.
Lovers should be explorers, along with Indians and old men.
I'll be the green sky, you be the star.
I'll make slight but eager moves toward you,
Eager also for clear stakes and garbled messages:
MUNDANE APE SCANS MUSIC STOP PAY FOR
  SELECTION STOP
BEWARE SMALL WINDS REGARDS P.A.L.
  RECORDING CO. STOP.
Over the years I've come to realize
And then drift back, as if a sweet scent
Was worth the trip. She'll go anywhere for a kiss
And so she will. I like the feel of no comparison.
I like the invisible pressure of some other time on time.

Like Moths to Flame

Posing, and allowing for a gala sagacity
To be nuptial and phantom, we ride the escaping sea
Without asking, so the sailors, habitually daring
And muscular, are marooned on the coast.
Perhaps all marriages are meant to break up,
To flail on the gradual heap of silent misgivings,
To tire of the menu. Glamor is unremitting.
The night is stark. If we cannot depict reality
Then how can we vow to make our way toward it?
We thought we might sail to Bali.
We thought we might find there an unsuspicious mob
Of daring and muscular daughters, who sing pleasantly
In makeshift shrines of braided rope and jasmine.
Already I sense a lethal snag: too many bugs,
A sudden allergy to fish, and besides
We have squandered the exotic
So that all the four-star places are reserved
For the past. Every now and then, a stray day
Finds its way to the surface of our unguarded desires
And we couple with it, wrecking all precedent, gaining ground.

Second Descent, Again

Wooden crate pulled deftly apart,
Thin paper set loose. This
While the tome is balanced
Between your wife and not your wife, while
The requiem doles out illusions of return.
Sanctus. Curious. Delirium.
Double scar in the far sky: star, star.
She said, "I haven't yearned since April."

Surcease, purview. Nothing so for miles
And now night. Lost sight of
Noon's hollow girth, clam shells, fitted,
Everything on edge. Days when light
Hoops, a low band
On which some of us stand ready and willing
To slip past the look just before the end.
"Only for a certain amount of time are we wanted."

Then? Well then
We have it in mind to climb something steep
And to wear a hat. We have it in mind
To cross paths with those no longer recognized:
Distant cousin, daughter of a long-dead friend.
She writes impressions of birdsongs for single violin.
All is forgotten. "After the war, we . . ." All is forgotten.

Closing Hours

This trace, if it exists, is alms for delusion.
An arch uncurls from the floor
Scented with the scent of a tapestry, housed here.
I recall the hour but not its passage
Unless dream captures and ties it to sleep:
A fat bellhop smiles, shows me to the tower
Where I can watch the departure.
But some days settle so that nothing
Crosses the horizon; stare as I will, no star
Needles the air. Now I am left
On the outskirts of a forest hemmed in by wheat
Where plump trees hide the image, its symmetry
Shot up and blown across the ground like feathers.
The unicorn, the grail, blue and red wings
Of kneeling musicians, these are embroidered
Elsewhere. Perseverance was crowned.
Hope and Pity prayed for success.
How fast is this camera? Can it record a trace?
There was a voyage. Four mounted horses
Strain against centuries.
To each is allotted: dust kicked up, smoke, plumage.

Monody

This utterance is not jazz,
Inspired by digression but loyal to fate,
Arriving back on time to meet up with song.
Left to its own devices, the soul is furtive,
Scavenging thrift to make ends meet:
Plays with Psyche's hair, pokes at the air
Where music is, talks to itself
As it waits for public transportation
To take it through a windy reverie or street.
Colloquies occur, bunched on the curb
Like marigolds no one picks
Or names that come to mind unattended.
It takes a route around revelation
Knowing you are in the next room
Where the screening is, where the scene shifts
Fatally as on the tip of my tongue
Or a dream that plummets into morning.
Last night we rode a pinwheel across the sea.
We kissed goodbye again and I think last words
Were said as I passed you the umbrella:
It was about to rain; I was about to wake up.
What happens gains momentum
But these forms are murderous in intent:
Contrived by oblivion, curtailed by release,
And now the narrative sky is sprayed with birds in flight.

Poem for Margrit, for Frida

The elusive recitation—
Blacks submerged in cold suds
Relaxed from shape, less
Hope or help than,
Dry, in heaps, on the black floor,
At the very least wearable—
The recitation abridged
So that panic and ardor
Are picked from a general sense
Of something depicted, some chord
Struck: the soldier's collar up
Against cold, or her heart
Submerged in the ruddy glow of paint
And weaponry or weeds piercing the shoulders
Where we expect to find neither flesh nor air.
In another ethos, wings would prevail.

In rare instances, the iconic
Is translated precisely:
Vocal, serene, if layered.
I write this way for mystery and need,
The images endeavoring to fold
Around a central nerve,
And to salvage what is worn from wear.

Day Dreams of Night

The day conveys its refusals
Not ever to guide the damned
Not ever to subside
From its only craft, that of going on
Inviolate, not even listening
When the heavy doves quicken and furnish,
Their care bequeathed to us
As instinct to desire.
                                    Duration
Is in the manner of skies,
Placidly innocent and stretched bodily
As, in the imagined sphere,
You lay down beside me, nearly here.
Volition is charmed by harmonies
Drawn around us in the unscented wind
And rendered physical, acting to assuage,
Tearing from us both place and departure.
                                              Now
We are stripped of usual change
And of declaration.
Then this day is about demeanor, how
The day evades its call to enlighten,
And so to let go.
The sky pours itself away.
I had hoped the thin dark
Would lift us above thaw, rupture,
Thefts from the night's foreground
Where colors keep their bounty far from home.

Before Recollection

Here we begin: not to let purposes transcend making.
All day in the shadow of, and then
To propose a critical approach to, love
Or color or the vindictive aspects of spring.
Descent is optional, even as we twine
In the vicinity of grace,
An aspect of mourning, hoping to find
Someone to help the heart without question.

There is another morning when we twine
In the center of grace, helpless,
And find emblems for now
And dream somewhat.
What is yours is mine, stacked
Against the season as allowance without thrift
So the requiem lifts hours to the sky,
Dilutes rose, then dries into night.
You say there is some place like never
But these trees resemble a former green
Held in abeyance, branched, becoming inordinate.

IV. A SIMPLE SERVICE

Medieval Evening

Earliness treads, curtailing momentum
But cool and lavish as wind:
Torpor vanished, myth reawakened.
As if surprise still lurked
Sucking at daylight, fundamental
To windows: trumpets, guardian saints,
A host of angels visible for once as fact
Even as we confuse murder with genius
And fulfill ourselves with the unfulfilled.
I grant you this face, these arms, this respite,
A merry-go-round spinning into night, ardent.
I grant you this battalion of blues
To ease you so that you might
Forgive the twilight its faint praise
Of an innate beauty, missed and retrieved daily.

Lake of Isles

Dimly perceived coast
Caressed where water is
Where lucid stretches finger belief
On occasion and the aftermath of occasion.
Seen from here, night is measured,
And stories no longer hold permanence.
Days adhere and a faint wind
Anoints our giving with something
Limitless: eddies pull and turn
Set loose in reaches where no harbor is.

If only I could regard the perpetual
As calm and slaked, not couched
In the unforeseen or
Tied into remnants
As if, having touched you once
I had touched you always
And could stay in the bonds of this lake
As part of a readiness: awakened, awake.

Topaz

Some treason we have come to know as
Belonging to pleasure, the way city streets
Invite deliverance, and all
The in-betweens we have come, also, to know.
Having, not having, slips between windows
Where plastic calf and sequined brow move,
Late on, to desire. Gradually, I admit
To wanting you, as if you
Were real, not just an arrangement with time.
Within each of us the autonomous declares,
Enters barefoot, turns off the lights, gives itself up.

Almost

Lined up against an old adage of the universe
With small feet, there are
Times which take paths
Unaccountably, and I am hardly able to walk
Near you, the place I have kept for you near me.
There are no memories for this encounter,
The objects have passed among many hands,
Are preserved in their own history.
The river where we swam is mere water.
And I want you to come toward me
To console me. I want you
To expect me as if I were the hour
That took us and shed us, rescinded and kept within.

A Simple Service

And now the day
Comes slowly on us, perfumed, cool,
Wherein amnesty and tide
Are part of what we thought was passing
But which is headed our way, bearing down,
About to seal us off
While the rest strut from cartoon to cartoon
Mouthing wisecracks and "phooey"
As the ditch, that place where things occur,
Fills to the rim with brine
And with the last peonies of the season.

The gentle guise that summer is
Is our right to pass, and for our sake
We have taken our cues from the garden,
Standing under the canopy with allegiance
To the calm voice speaking for us, blessing ash.
Always I had wanted to speak calmly
Like a landscape just after rain
When radiance is styled for perception
The day the last ancient is placed
Beside father, mother and brother
On a green afternoon overlooking life.
Those who remain are implied, being here now.

Inner Life

Speaking to me from there again.
The chairs lessened
After I had invited you here,
Sponsored your touch.
Prayer goes against the grain
But twice now the appeal has been set
Plainly, as a church vividly aspires
To be only where those who would could.
Dream has a bearing on this,
The way moments submit
Even when the essential place is gone,
Where the altar was,
Or not knowing how to look
Into your eyes directly
For fear sorrow would be
Quick to replace permission to stay.
Until now, lists have sufficed
Awaiting alleviation,
Each entry falling into the world
And freeing us a little, too little.
The season you so easily ignore is
Upon us, full of acreage, remorse
And avowal. Speaking to you from here again.

Path

                                What is
Is that you might declare
Characteristically,
By an assumed nearness or slope
Whose reason to be eager is also
The reticence you shield from entirety.
Under which I find myself cast.
Is this something like mercy,
The better solitude, when,
Attaching herself to the morning's press
She makes for herself a habit
From the simplest stuff, testing this
Agenda only? And if not, why not?
The occasion is meant to be witnessed.
Blade after blade, the curve delves.

In this way urgency wells,
Nicknamed history, but in fact
A slow banquet taking place down by the sea
Or lake or, since it is essential,
Any place that tells of itself evenings.
It is in my interest to follow
Although you are nowhere
To be seen. You know where.

Vernal Elegy

in memoriam Constance Ernst Bessie

Crammed into a corner, the heart
Does no good to swell
Into another image: the sea
Listing too easily; hard buds
Breathing into their mute precocity
Even as we give our best love freely
Over the counter, an announcement
In the here and now.
                                    Wind
Might leave a legacy also,
Slants and shreds as well as deeper abrasions
On the face, and the dunes ride high
And the cliffs stay. Ping!
The smallest sphere collides, dispersing
There surely to change what is recoverable.
Those who are told can't tell.
Only those who knew now know.

The Vanquished

A deeper sun
Saying this mirth, this imperfect grappling
With underpinnings.
Toothless, smiling: a rind.
Or, organized never again to predict,
The most sequestered is
Aroused, and so shown to be explicit
After all. Summoned from the inequalities
Of daring, ourselves, exampling,
Manage to find our way to the well
Where unsafe foothills
And insurmountable calligraphies
Rinse upward.
                        We search for apt signatures
Where they aren't, the names
Bathed out of reach
As when invention immerses fact.
I mean the way she hurried to meet him
And was almost too late, as
I hurry and am too late
Because here it is
Falling across without benediction
Or wanly imagined, as in these jars
Lovely with dry things. After a while
The seasons, turning, twitch,
No longer sedated, nor expectant,
Uneasily seeded.

Subject to Change

Those of us who are there will never leave.
Given our inability to make a version,
One that does not twist
Off the ground, the same ground we have
Imagined, separately,
The thing casts itself into being.
Such impediments cannot be altered.
Other ideas are lost.
Are they ideas? What thing?
Once there was possibility
But now that too is gone
Predicting the river.
Is it all, and will it stay
Longer than usual,
Gathering hesitancy only because it
Is new, until, heavily absorbent,
Boundaries fail, as if of ash?
The sky was something else, massive
But kind, leaving nothing in its wake.
Often I have thought the linear
Duplicitous, mapping outer and inner,
Showing us core and enclosure
As it helps itself over destiny's rail.
The difference is the air's lunar kiss,
A residual, if despondent, bearing.
Those of us who leave were never there.

Aperture

It does not come as hairline fractures
Mapping plaster with brittle rivers
Nor with the unmeasured gait
Of a tulip's averting grace
(Lathed to half-rhyme with death)
While these others, these anemones,
Peel back Padua's choir of angels
Plummeting and stayed, frescoes of disbelief
That came only by faith, never by description
Which cannot save despite its comforts
As we might say: touch me here,
Put your hand here where it hurts. Where
Is it? What is the unimaginable source of it?
This transparent stain left on the air where was is.

Coastal

This sort of thing happens.
The implausible converts under pressure
The pressure of night carriers
Who begin to sing
In flat territories of the central region.
I suppose all awakenings serve to refresh,
Even then the place is untraveled or
Afternoon after afternoon
Depleted uniquely.
But some mornings usurp
Sleepless meanwhiles
When conjuring begins
Far under the tower of lights.
And so goes elsewhere, climbs
The steep coast road above the village
Giddy and starkly obedient. Below,
The Adriatic is the same as the beautiful
And the will comes back to make it
Out of the thing stressed almost into being.
Or look away, into the rock.

Sacred Weather

1. OCTOBER LAKE

The lake, riddled with wind, splinters
Into raglan grass, upright as staves
Fending expansion or extending vestigial guard
To a small, solitary duck: winter's decoy.
Yesterday a ragged line of geese
(The same as Monday, trafficked down
And swam and fed, bottoms up
Like sudden buoys, then left like thankless
Relatives) headed south to longevity: they
Rent the sky which, today, is
Too deeply set to be mere cloud: a whole season
Packed above and ready to be delivered.

Beneath the ridge, east across the lake,
Shadow meanders with an elegant melancholia,
Velvet bunched then swept aside
On Pre-Raphaelite wing, a shift in tide
Or else the sighting of someone who also saw,
Three dawns ago, doe and fawn
In silhouette break the mirrored sun;
The one who saw Venus rising.
The foreground is in a jittery recitative,
Girlish and alarmed, while beyond a great processional
Once more chorales the brilliant ruin.

2. MAPLE, MOON, JAY

This fidgeting is prelude and effect.
Less and less substantial, gold and broken,
Shade is an old wheel stirring underfoot
With access to nothing but gust.
A gathered dispersal, as when
That other moon
Lengthens in plumes of held water.
Then distance is a charm
Imperfectly sent down the plumb line
Into light's incoherent but accurate twin.

Night water is a smudge of timing
Surrounded by small illusions
Lifted into the visible.
What is it to find these valuables
Just as everything is about to sleep?
A remnant blue rips and flies dreamward
Onto satin wrapped around my father
Whose sleeve was last seen bound to a wing.

3. The Meadow

An almost intolerable dusk.
It is a weave and it is
A hollow blanketing.
When air leaps there is a scan
Loosely applied to direction
And the sky collapses
Its fable on water, as if on water,
Raising the hackles of grass into shadow.
Death by seeing.
Cold rusts into the slope
And the deer, also, have darkened.
The furthest cold; its most rigid appeal.
Exposure is a ubiquitous curfew
Under three nights of hunter's moon
Beamed onto this:
A hoodlum misfit expert stalking.

4. THE CHAMBER

As I lay in the sky
A small blade opened the night.

The pines have turned.
Now yellowish pinnacles
Rain newly matte footing
As if all our sun had fallen to mangers.

As I lie in the night
A small star opens the sky.

5. MOONRISE, RAIN

Evening's certain reduction is also a conduit:
Radiance muted, in balance, and
Poised, a rubbing, air surfaced on the lake,
While nearby early episodes linger.
Nevertheless a darkening ensues,
Its linearity softened as if by deception.
The far stretch is a limit or shore:
Curiously intimate pale grass;
The start of another season.
Chandeliers hang and crest, their light
Turned loose to a weightless hurry
Harvested, as silence is in seclusion.
Then, all this absorbed,
A geometry forms, plowing a new route to radiance.

Intimacy is sometimes deceptive,
A weightless hurry to avoid darkening.
Evening's geometry softens,
Lingering in the loosely turning lake.
The stillness absorbs all this:
Chandeliers, harvest, and silence
Routed through another season.
Seclusion's reduction is also a conduit.
Nevertheless a balance forms, its crest
The start of radiance like that grassy limit
Or shore. Certain early episodes rub,
Curiously nearby, poised to ensue.
A pale linearity hangs a new surface in the air
Like a mute plow stretching the light.

71

6. SACRED WEATHER

Mist heals, rain scrims its way
To cooler portions, claims
What inveterate sorrow the eyes restrain.
The unbroken mute pictorial vase
Its virtuous stillness turned
Inward along shell lines, baffles to shore.
Lovely ephemera, guide
Air to ear: here lies the reliquary tide.

Many have ceased to pine.
Stasis is an attribute, domain of the lily.
Even the sky gives color up,
An ecstasy too slight, less than free.
I myself long to refrain
But would bleed and bless
Robe opening on slowly mounted stair.

NOTE

I owe special thanks to the following people, who gave invaluable support and guidance along the way: Deborah Baker, William Elton, Leslie Miller, Bradford Morrow, Charles Molesworth, Jeannette Watson Sanger, and Marjorie Welish. Particular gratitude is due to Yaddo, where a number of these poems were written.

Some of these poems were initially dedicated to friends. I would not like those dedications to be lost. They are "Bridgehampton 1950, 1980" for Darragh Park; "Transcendental Postcard" for Joe Brainard; "Moonlight in Calais" for Kenward Elmslie; "An Aura of Abstraction Gives Way" for Louisa Chase; "In the Garden" for my brother, David; "Mimetic" for Peter Minichiello; "Here and There" for Hector Leonardi; "Some Other Time" for Paul Auster; "Day Dreams of Night" for Martin Earl; and "Before Recollection" for Brian Conley.

Other poems were written partly in response to paintings and photographs, and I would like to acknowledge the artists. They are: Louisa Chase ("Café Acute"); Pablo Picasso ("Portrait"); Jan Groover ("Still Life with Apricots"); Robert Moskowitz ("Carousel"); Margrit Lewczuk ("Poem for Margrit, for Frida"); Bill Jensen ("The Vanquished"); and Thomas Nozkowski ("Subject to Change").

73